THE TRUTHER FILES

Skeptic's Book of Secrets, Lies, False Flags, Cover-Ups and Conspiracies

by Horace Martin Woodhouse
Author of *Anatomy of an Assassination*

"A lie told often enough becomes the truth."
— Vladimir Lenin

"The bigger the lie, the more it will be believed."
— Joseph Goebbels

"A lie would have no sense unless the truth
were felt dangerous."
— Alfred Adler

In Pursuit of the F*cking Truth

Merriam-Webster's Collegiate Dictionary defines a conspiracy theory as "a theory that explains an event or set of circumstances as the result of a secret plot by usually powerful conspirators." Conspiracy theories posit that "a group is acting in secret to alter institutions, usurp power, hide truth or gain utility at the expense of the common good."

This is an age of power and deception. We live in a world where the powerful deceive us. Control of what we watch, read, and hear by a few unaccountable men of influence breeds distrust, which gives rise to alternative, often contradictory, explanations. Supreme Court justice Louis Brandeis called sunlight the best disinfectant, and what many might dismiss as conspiracy theories bring daylight where there used to be darkness, shedding light on arguable thought and action. Conspiracy theories are ultimately beneficial because they reveal actual anomalies in mainstream explanations and demand greater transparency from governments and institutions. And censorship by control or suppression of what would otherwise constitute investigative journalism plays into the conspiracy theorist's notion that powerful forces bury information that challenges conventional wisdom.

Conspiracy theories provide individuals with a public opportunity, otherwise likely denied to them, of addressing the credibility of governments or other socio-political actors. So-called conspiracies must be recognized as attempts to map, in narrative form, the trajectories and effects of power. Clearly, people and governments have conspired against each other, throughout human history. Healthy skepticism lies at the very heart of the scientific endeavor.

Sociologist Theodore Sasson states, "Conspiracy theories explain disturbing events or social phenomena in terms of the actions of specific, powerful individuals." In his view, conspiracy theories may be regarded as the beginnings of social movements that could create positive change and foster solidarity. Mark Fenster, a law professor and the author of *Conspiracy Theories: Secrecy and Power in American Culture*, believes a sense of conspiracy is "almost an instinctive response to strange events." And according to political science professor Joanne M. Miller, "to the extent that conspiracy theories fill a need for certainty, it is thought they may gain more widespread acceptance in instances when establishment or mainstream explanations contain erroneous information, discrepancies, or ambiguities." A conspiracy theory, in this sense, helps explain those ambiguities and provides a convenient alternative to living with uncertainty.

When conventional truth is not the only story, the truth deserves another look. We're surrounded by a tornado of controversial events and possible cover-ups, and a lot remains to be done in researching the history, structure and dynamics of conspiracy theories. This book takes up the challenge, guiding the reader on a trip through the world's most intriguing secrets, lies, false flags, cover-ups and machinations of powerful actors, supported by follow-up materials culled from online news sources, blogs, and websites.

Bilderberg Group

An annual conference established in 1954 by Prince Bernhard of the Netherlands, ostensibly intended to "foster dialogue between Europe and North America," the Bilderberg Group includes bankers, politicians, directors of large businesses and board members from large publicly traded corporations, including IBM, Xerox, Royal Dutch Shell, Nokia and Daimler. Controversial statesman Henry Kissinger is a regular, while Bill Clinton, Bill Gates, and Christine Lagarde, and more recently, Commerce Secretary Wilbur Ross and former National Security Adviser H.R. McMaster have attended. But the meetings lack reasonable transparency and accountability, and the group has been accused of conspiring to impose capitalist domination, world government, and a planned economy. Some claim the Group controls the European Union and intends to create a Fourth Reich. One Bilderberg objective is to de-industrialize the world by suppressing scientific development, starting in the United States.

Further Reading: Estulin, Daniel, *The True Story of the Bilderberg Group*, TrineDay Publishing, 2009.

Censorship by Google

Big Tech has been historically associated with West Coast liberalism and Democratic politics, and Conservatives are certain that Silicon Valley despises them, that its Stanford-trained engineers regard the Right with ridicule and hostility. While Google, Facebook and Twitter have all emphatically denied any technological anti-Conservative bias, research shows otherwise. Since these companies ensure that their practices remain undisclosed, there is no way of definitively proving that algorithmic anti-Conservative bias exists from the outside. Yet powerful and persuasive research validates speculation that technology companies are encoding anti-conservative bias into the architecture of their businesses. For example, in August 2018, Paula Bolyard, a supervising editor at the Conservative news outlet PJ Media, published a story reporting that 96% of Google search results for Donald Trump prioritized "left-leaning and anti-Trump media outlets."

Further Reading: Nazaryan, Alexander (March 15, 2018) Is Silicon Valley Silencing Conservatives on Social Media? <www.newsweek.com>

Frey Effect

Cornell University neuroscientist Allan H. Frey was the first American to identify the microwave auditory effect, a human perception of audible clicks, or even speech, induced by pulsed or modulated radio frequencies. Individuals suffering from auditory hallucinations have claimed that government agents use forms of mind control technologies based on microwave signals to transmit sounds and thoughts into their heads as a form of electronic harassment. During the Cold War, Washington suspected that the Soviets were working on turning microwave radiation into covert weapons of mind control. These unconventional weapons may have caused the perception of loud noises, including ringing, buzzing and grinding that, starting in late 2016, harmed American diplomats in Cuba and China. Symptoms included nausea, crushing headaches, fatigue, dizziness, sleep problems and hearing loss. The medical team that studied the Cuba diplomats ascribed the symptoms to "an unknown energy source" that was highly directional.

Further Reading: Broad, William J. (September 1, 2018) Microwave Weapons Are Prime Suspect in Ills of U.S. Embassy Workers. <www.nytimes.com>

Great Replacement

In a deliberate scheme, the global and liberal elite of the European Union plan to allow as many as 15 million new migrants to enter Europe in the coming years, a planned replacement of European peoples, literally changing the faces of these countries. The imminent danger of European culture, civilization, and identity being overrun by unhindered mass migration has become known as the Great Replacement. The white Catholic population and white Christian European population at large are being systematically replaced with non-European people, specifically Middle Eastern, North and Sub-Saharan African populations, through mass migration and demographic growth. According to mathematical models, progressing Islamization will cause the disappearance of Europeans in their own countries. In a preview of the Great Replacement, the 1973 novel *Le Camp des Saints* by Jean Raspail depicts the collapse of Western culture owing to an overwhelming "tidal wave" of Third World immigration.

Further Reading: Williams, Thomas Chatterton (December 4, 2017). The French Origins of "You Will Not Replace Us." *The New Yorker* <www.newyorker.com>

Flat Earth

Members of the Flat Earth Society believe that "round Earth" is a fabrication orchestrated by NASA and other government agencies. They insist Earth is a flat disc with the Arctic Circle in the center and Antarctica, a 150-foot-tall wall of ice around the rim to prevent inhabitants from falling off. Since the surface of water cannot curve, the oceans must be flat all the way across. And if Earth was spherical, an airplane flying above would need to constantly adjust its nose downward to avoid flying straight out into space. GPS devices, they believe, are being rigged in order to make airplane pilots think they are flying around a sphere when they are actually flying in circles above the disc. The Bedford Level Experiment is a series of observations carried out along a six-mile length of the Old Bedford River in the United Kingdom to measure the curvature of the Earth. Samuel Birley Rowbotham, who conducted the first observations in 1838, claimed he had proven the Earth to be flat.

Further Reading: <www.theflatearthsociety.org>

Black Helicopters

It is believed that silent-running black helicopters or "phantom helicopters" are in use by troops of a secret shadow government. Since the 1960s, these mysterious helicopters, lacking any identifying markings, have been reported near areas of UFO sightings, alien abduction claims, and cattle mutilations. Black helicopters are also thought to have a connection with men dressed in black suits working for unknown organizations who have threatened UFO witnesses to keep them quiet about what they have seen. While most U.S. Army helicopters are painted a dark olive color, helicopters stealthy enough to penetrate airspace and operate undetected, are painted black. Despite clear evidence, the U.S. government has never acknowledged the existence of these helicopters. *The Las Vegas Review-Journal* reported that the radar-evading stealth technology used by the MH-60 Black Hawk helicopters in the raid on Osama bin Laden's compound was developed in the early 1990s at Area 51.

Further Reading: Rogers, Keith (May 7, 2011). Stealth craft in bin Laden raid has Nevada ties. *Las Vegas Review-Journal.* <www.reviewjournal.com>

Brookings Report

The 1960 report, officially established for the study of communications systems, weather predicting systems, space industry, and foreign policy, has become controversial for one section, an evaluation of potential public reaction to contact with intelligent extraterrestrial life, and under what circumstances leaders might withhold such information from the public. *The Brookings Report* suggests that contact with extraterrestrial life could have a disruptive effect on human societies. It warns that, of all groups, "scientists and engineers might be the most devastated by the discovery of relatively superior creatures, since these professions are most clearly associated with the mastery of nature, rather than with the understanding and expression of man. Advanced understanding of nature might vitiate all our theories at the very least, if not also require a culture and perhaps a brain inaccessible to earth scientists." NASA has been accused of covering up evidence of extraterrestrial civilization already discovered on the Moon, the planet Mars, and possibly elsewhere in the solar system.

Further Reading: Dews, Fred (May 12, 2014). Communications, Technology, and Extraterrestrial Life: The Advice Brookings Gave NASA about the Space Program in 1960. <www.brookings.edu>

Denver Airport

On February 28, 1995, Denver International Airport opened to the public after falling over a year behind schedule and spending $2 billion more than its original budget. Some theorists believe the delay and overrun were due to construction of a secret subterranean city, intended to serve as headquarters of an emerging totalitarian world government, with tunnels and secret bunkers meant to house world leaders during a worldwide catastrophe. A dedication marker at the airport indicates it was funded by "The New World Airport Commission," but no such group seems to exist. Adding fuel to that fire, artwork found throughout the building portray Masonic or Satanic symbols, and a set of murals, some of which depict a world of destruction and decay, others a utopian vision of the future. The airport entrance is inexplicably guarded by a sculpture locals call "Blucifer," a demonic 32-foot blue horse rearing in rage. If viewed from the air, the DIA runways are revealed to be laid out in the shape of a Nazi swastika.

Further Reading: Erbland, Kate (February 8, 2016) 5 Conspiracy Theories Surrounding the Denver Airport. <www.mentalfloss.com>

Sasquatch Encounters

It is believed that the dense forests of the American/Canadian northwest provide habitat to human-like creatures called Sasquatch, confirmed in 1980 when the government secretly removed burned Sasquatch corpses from Mount St. Helens after the destructive volcanic eruption. Following the disaster, witnesses reported seeing federal helicopters carrying away charred remains of several Sasquatches from the area. Prior to the eruption, Mount St. Helens had already been a hot spot for supposed "ape-men" sightings since the 1920s. The evasiveness and isolationist behavior of these creatures has been attributed to their ability to hibernate for very long periods of time after feeding seasons. Also called "Bigfoot," its enormous footprints are claimed to be as large as 24 inches long and 8 inches wide. Ape Canyon, a gorge on the southeast shoulder of Mount St. Helens, is the site of a violent encounter in 1924 between a group of miners and a group of apemen, as reported in the July 16, 1924 issue of *The Oregonian*.

Further Reading: Perry, Douglas (January 25, 2018) How a 1924 Bigfoot battle on Mt. St. Helens helped launch a legend. *The Oregonian*.

Alternate Chronology

According to Russian mathematician Anatoly Fomenko's theory of New Chronology, the conventional measurement of time periods in Middle Eastern and European history is fundamentally flawed, and events attributed to the civilizations of the Roman Empire, Ancient Greece and Ancient Egypt actually occurred during the Middle Ages, more than a thousand years later. According to Fomenko, the written history of the human race goes only as far back as 800 AD, since there is almost no information about events between 800 to 1000 AD, and most known historical events took place from 1000 to 1500 AD. He believes that world history was deliberately falsified for political reasons and that documents that conflict with New Chronology have been edited or fabricated by the Vatican, the Holy Roman Empire, and the Romanoff dynasty. Fomenko's theories have been endorsed by several other prominent Russians, including former chess champion Garry Kasparov.

Further Reading: Kuroski, John (April 24, 2018) Why Anatoly Fomenko's New Chronology Says That "History" Is All A Fake. <www.allthatsinteresting.com>

Uranium One

Hillary Clinton was Secretary of State at the time the State Department agreed to approve a deal to sell a Canadian company to the Russian atomic energy agency. Known as Uranium One, the company's global uranium mining stakes included 20 percent of the uranium production capacity in the United States. As the Russians gradually assumed control of Uranium One in three separate transactions from 2009 to 2013, Canadian records show a flow of cash making its way to the Clinton Foundation, contributions not publicly disclosed by the Clintons despite an agreement Hillary Clinton had struck with the Obama White House, placing limits on the activities of her husband's foundation. Shortly after the Russians announced their intention to acquire a majority stake in Uranium One, Mr. Clinton received $500,000 for a Moscow speech from a Russian investment bank with links to the Kremlin. The deal put Vladimir Putin closer to his goal of controlling much of the global uranium supply chain.

Further Reading: Becker, Jo and McIntire, Mike (April 23, 2015) Cash Flowed to Clinton Foundation Amid Russian Uranium Deal. *The New York Times.*

The Tunguska Event

On the morning of June 30, 1908, a large explosion occurred near the Tunguska River over a sparsely populated region of Easter Siberia. The explosion, generally attributed to the air burst of a meteor, completely obliterated and deforested everything within a several hundred mile radius, yet since no impact crater has ever been found, the meteor is thought to have disintegrated before ever hitting the surface of the Earth. The event remains shrouded in mystery, in part because scientists themselves cannot decide what actually happened, and after many decades of intensive investigations they have yet to find a single identifiable remnant of the object. In 1946, Soviet writer Alexander Kazantsev proposed an alternative explanation, which has taken hold and spawned generations of true believers in Russia. He suggested that the huge explosion was caused by the crash of an alien spaceship. Others have theorized that Nicola Tesla's experimental power transmitter in Shoreham, New York was the cause of the Tunguska Event.

Further Reading: Paoletti, Gabe (December 1, 2017) The Mysterious Tunguska Event That Baffles Scientists To This Day. <www.allthatsinteresting.com>

Gay Bomb

In 1994, the Wright Laboratory in Ohio, predecessor to the U.S. Air Force Research Laboratory, proposed the production of a variety of non-lethal chemical weapons. One specific request was made for funds to pursue the development of a weapon that would turn enemy combatants gay. The so-called Gay Bomb would theoretically discharge female sex pheromones over enemy forces in order to make them sexually attracted to each other. The aphrodisiac chemical was expected to provoke widespread homosexual behavior among militants, causing what the strategists called a "distasteful but completely non-lethal" blow to morale. It is speculated that the actual development and clandestine use of this technology explains the growth of the gay population. Secret documents are said to show that the government has fostered homosexuality with "estrogen mimickers" placed in juice boxes and water bottles to "feminize" people, thereby limiting population growth.

Further Reading: Glaister, Dan (July 13, 2007). Air Force looked at spray to turn enemy gay. *The Guardian*.

Osama bin Laden

"Justice," said President Obama in a televised address to the nation, "has been done." Yet reports on the killing of Osama bin Laden fall somewhere between fantasy and mythology. We are asked to believe that Obama sent 23 SEALs on a seemingly suicidal mission, invading Pakistani air space without air or ground cover, into a compound that, if it even contained bin Laden, by all rights should have been heavily guarded. Doubts about bin Laden's death were fueled by the U.S. military's supposed disposal of his body at sea, the decision to not release any photographic or DNA evidence, and a 25-minute blackout during the raid. Although the raid has been described in great detail by U.S. officials, no physical evidence constituting actual proof of his death has been offered to the public. It is suspected that bin Laden had been killed a number of years earlier in the Tora Bora mountains, but that this information had been kept secret to encourage continued support for the war on terror.

Further Reading: Mahler, Jonathan (October 15, 2015) What Do We Really Know About Osama bin Laden's Death? *The New York Times* <www.nytimes.com>

Zermatism

According to the theory of Zermatism, all human culture has its origin at Easter Island following the Deluge which killed all living beings except those on Noah's Ark. The doctrine maintains that all languages are derived from a single source known as the Protong, and all cultures are just a variation of the themes representing a series of universal symbols. The theory was conceived by an eccentric genius named Stanislav Szukalski who was born in Gidle in Poland around 1893 and died in Burbank, California in 1987. In his view, humanity was locked in an eternal struggle with the Sons of Yeti, the offspring of Yeti and humans, and differences in races and cultures were due primarily to inter-species breeding between near -perfect ancestral beings and the humanoid creatures. He claimed that the figures of the god Pan on Greek vases depict creatures that actually existed, the product of Yeti apes raping human women. Szukalski wrote over 10,000 pages about Zermatism and illustrated his argument with 40,000 illustrations.

Further Reading: Ollman, Leah (November 20, 2000) Intense "Struggle" Sums Up Artist's Hyperbolic Style. *Los Angeles Times.*

FEMA Camps

The government agency tasked with management of major emergencies within the country, including ensuring the continuity of government during a large-scale disaster, FEMA has been operating behind the scenes to prepare an action in case of an American revolt that will not only squash a revolution, but kill many of its participants. The theory in general states that once a disaster or threat of one comes into being, martial law will be declared and FEMA's emergency powers will come into operation. The first step of this action would be to disarm the American people and throw anyone that is, or might be, a threat into a detention center. FEMA has set up several concentration camps around the country in preparation for the imposition of martial law, and with the expectation that many will die in a revolt, the agency has stored 500,000 plastic coffins around the country. The internment of Japanese Americans during World War II in specifically constructed camps is evidence that such a scenario has historic precedent.

Further Reading: Graff, Garrett M. (September 3, 2017) The Secret History of FEMA. <www.wired.com>

Q Anon

On October 28, 2017, an anonymous person, identifying as "Q Clearance Patriot," posted an online message titled "The Calm Before the Storm." Q established his legend as a government insider with top security clearance who knew the truth about the Trump administration and its opponents in the United States. In a series of cryptic messages Q accused numerous liberal Hollywood actors, politicians, and high-ranking officials of engaging in an international child sex trafficking ring and explained that Donald Trump feigned collusion with Russians in order to enlist Robert Mueller in an effort to expose the ring and prevent a coup by Barack Obama, Hillary Clinton, and George Soros. Q has alleged that U.S. Representative and former Democratic National Committee chairwoman Debbie Wasserman Schultz hired El Salvadorian gang MS-13 to murder DNC staffer Seth Rich, that German Chancellor Angela Merkel is the granddaughter of Adolf Hitler, and that the Rothschilds are leaders of a satanic cult.

Further Reading: Darby, Luke (August 7, 2018) What the Hell Is QAnon? The Right-Wing Conspiracy Theory, Explained. *Gentleman's Quarterly* <www.gq.com>

Barcodes

Technology of the optical, machine-readable barcode was founded in 1949 and became widespread after 1981 when the Department of Defense adopted its use for marking all products sold to the U.S. military. Barcodes now link potential buyers with items that are offered for sale throughout the commercial financial system, allowing the entire economy to be electronically linked and identified through a system of marks. In chapter 13, verse 17 of the Bible's Book of Revelation, which predicts the apocalypse, the author, John the Apostle, writes that "no man might buy or sell, save he that had the mark, or the name of the beast, or the number of his name." Some have proposed that barcodes are actually intended to serve as means of control by a putative world government, or that they are Satanic in intent. The claim is based on the assumption that the digit 6 is encoded as 101 (bar-space-bar), then the longer guard bars at the left, right, and middle can be interpreted as 666, the Mark of the Beast.

Further Reading: Sullivan, Amy (November 28, 2012) Are Texas Schools Forcing Students to Bear the Mark of the Antichrist? <www.newrepublic.com>

Fort Knox

President Franklin Roosevelt commissioned the construction of Fort Knox in the mid-1930s, reportedly because the Treasury worried that U.S. gold reserves would not be safe from an enemy invasion. The 147.3 million ounces of gold that the government says are stored in Fort Knox are secured in what is considered to be the most impregnable building in the world. While the official story is that the gold has been in the massive vault for decades, many wonder if this is really the truth. There has been no audit of the actual gold since 1953 when Dwight D. Eisenhower was president, and during the audit, only 5 percent of the gold was tested, and no independent experts were used. There are many who claim that the Federal Reserve doesn't want a proper audit because the gold is not there, at least not all of it. Some groups believe that as part of its effort to manipulate the economy, the Federal Reserve has sold the gold. They speculate that the gold bars are actually tungsten bricks painted to look like the precious metal.

Further Reading: Rickards, James (August 23, 2017) The Truth About the Fort Knox Gold.

Cataclysmic Pole Shift

The Earth's true poles are not the same as its magnetic poles. This means that if you took two trips 10 years apart to the North Magnetic Pole by following a compass, you would end up at a different destination each time. Research shows that during the last 200 million years a total true polar wander of some 30 degrees has occurred, but no super-rapid shifts in the Earth's pole have been detected — until recently. Magnetic North has been moving at a rate of 31 miles a year since the last update in 2015, a faster than usual dash toward Siberia. In 1948, Hugh Auchincloss Brown, an electrical engineer, warned of the consequences of a catastrophic pole shift. Brown argued that climate change, earthquakes, volcanic eruptions, floods and tectonic events would result from stresses on the Earth's crust during a radical shift, and with the recent evidence of precession and changes in axial tilt, some claim that the Earth will soon experience a cataclysmic polar shift, and entire continents might sink while new ones emerge from the sea.

Further Reading: Seidel, Jamie (January 12, 2019) Earth's magnetic pole is on the move, fast. And we don't know why. <www.news.com.au>

California Wildfires

Tens of thousands of acres of private woodlands in California are being destroyed by wildfires as the state gets warmer, winters get shorter and fuel gets drier. Yet there's something unusual about fires that get larger and more damaging each year. The unprecedented scale of the devastation, together with certain anomalies observed during the fires and unexplained damage patterns, have prompted the widespread proliferation of theories about the cause. The fires may not in fact be caused by wind patterns, brutally dry conditions, the effects of climate change, or possible downed power lines, but by a sinister scheme directed by nefarious elements within the government. One theory is that "directed energy weapons" or government-directed lasers are bent on destroying homes and property, meant to clear the way for high-speed rail. The idea that the fires were created to make way for a rail line rests primarily on a graphic that purports to compare the areas damaged by fire with the layout of a proposed California high speed rail system.

Further Reading: Gutierrez, Melody (November 15, 2018) California's rush to start building high-speed rail sent costs

Wingdings Font

Developed in 1990 as fonts which render letters as a variety of symbols, Microsoft called the series "Wingdings" to combine an old printing term, "dingbat." with "Windows." In 1992, it was discovered that the character sequence "NYC" in Wingdings was a skull and crossbones symbol, a Star of David, and a thumbs-up gesture. A 1992 article in *The New York Post* even proclaimed, in screaming headlines, "Millions of computers carry a secret message that urges death to Jews in New York City!" Microsoft strongly denied this was intentional, and insisted that the final arrangement of the glyphs in the font was largely random. Then, in the wake of the September 11 terrorist attacks on New York's World Trade Center, theorists claim that the font contained the prediction that 9/11 would happen. In addition, when the airline flight number Q33NY is typed into Wingdings, it comes up with a plane, followed by two symbols which look like the Twin Towers then a skull and crossbones and the Star of David.

Further Reading: McAteer, Oliver (September 11, 2017) People think Wingdings predicted 9/11 with hidden messages. <www.metro.co.uk>

Crop Circles

The mysterious patterns in farmers' fields began appearing in the 1970s as simple circles in the English countryside. The number and complexity of the circles increased dramatically, reaching a peak in the 1980s and 1990s when more elaborate circles were produced, including those illustrating complex mathematical equations. The cause of many of the circles is unknown, and some crop circles have been proven to be hoaxes. The "saucer nests" of Tully, a small town in Australia, are the most famous circles known before the modern era, and Tully has become famous as a UFO tourist attraction, Australia's equivalent to Roswell. According to Dr. Horace Drew, molecular biologist at the California Institute of Technology, a number of the crop circles are legitimate and contain puzzles that can be decoded and linked to time travel and alien life. He claims that international media has played a part in causing the public to doubt the legitimacy of crop circles and the U.S. government knows much more about extraterrestrial life than it has publicly revealed.

Further Reading: Redford, Benjamin (June 9, 2017) The Crop Circle Mystery: A Closer Look.

Free Energy Suppression

Because everything is related to energy, if energy were free, there would be no more electric or oil bills. That possibility has spooked greedy manipulators of the petroleum industry and global financial system since the mid-19th century, and has led to the suppression of pre-existing unconventional energy sources. That claim is most significantly supported by the quashing of Nicola Tesla's work at the Wardenclyffe Tower in Shoreham, New York, an effort to produce limitless and free power by creating a channel between the Earth and the ionosphere for anyone to tap into. Much of Tesla's life was about providing free energy to the masses via wireless waves with no wires or ground infrastructure. Corporations will not allow anything to infringe on their stranglehold on the world's economy, suppressing all technologically viable, pollution-free, no-cost energy sources including perpetual motion machines, cold fusion generators, torus-based generators, as well as Tesla's unfulfilled vision of wireless energy transmission.

Further Reading: Walia, Arjun (October 11, 2013) Multiple Scientists Confirm The Reality of Free Energy. <www.collective-evolution.com>

Chemtrails

Contrails, or condensation trails, are streaks of condensed water vapor created in the air by an aircraft at high altitudes and under certain atmospheric conditions. Some contrails include chemical or biological agents deliberately sprayed at high altitude for some undisclosed purpose. Beginning in the late 1990s, the Air Force has been spraying the U.S. population with mysterious substances from aircraft, generating unusual patterns, and while normal contrails dissipate relatively quickly, chemtrails can be distinguished from contrails by their long duration, persisting for as much as a half day or transforming into cirrus-like clouds. It is suspected that contrails that linger contain additional substances, and the purpose of the chemical release may be solar radiation management, weather modification, psychological manipulation, human population control, or biological or chemical warfare. The trails, it is claimed, are to blame for health problems and respiratory illness.

Further Reading: Séguin, Xavier (January 18, 2018) Chemtrails: NASA Unmasked. <www.eden-saga.com>

Black Knight Satellite

The origin of the Black Knight dates back to extraterrestrial sources heard during the 1899 radio experiments of Nikola Tesla, and long-delayed echoes first heard by amateur radio operator Jørgen Hals in Oslo, Norway, in 1928. In February 1960, *Time Magazine* reported that the U.S. Navy had detected a dark object thought to be a Soviet spy satellite in orbit, and three years later, astronaut Gordon Cooper reported a UFO sighting during his 15th orbit in Mercury 9 and confirmed by international tracking stations. According to Scottish author Duncan Lunan, what Tesla heard and what Cooper saw was a spacecraft of extraterrestrial origin which has orbited Earth in near-polar orbit for approximately 13,000 years. He suggested that the probe may have originated from a planet located in the solar system of star Epsilon Boötis. A 1998 NASA photo is believed by some to show the Black Knight satellite, but NASA has stated that this is likely space debris, specifically a thermal blanket lost during an EVA mission.

Further Reading: Andrews, Stefan (August 19, 2018) Alien Satellite or Space Debris? Theories on the Dark Object Orbiting Earth Known as the "Black Knight."

Mass Shootings

It is believed by some that powerful forces are at work, routinely arranging massacres and terrorist atrocities to make it appear as if some other individual or group did them, in order to achieve their political goals. As school massacres spark debate and increase calls for tighter gun controls, could it be that mass shootings are actually orchestrated by the government as an excuse to restrict the sale of firearms? Wearing a gas mask and spraying bullets from an AR-15 assault rifle bought legally, Nikolas Cruz fired on former teachers and classmates at Marjory Stoneman Douglas High School in Parkland, Florida. Some of the survivors of the event are behind "March for Our Lives," a movement for gun control, leading to accusations they are not really students but "crisis actors" working for anti-gun groups who travel around the country to the sites of mass shootings. If the government or other agencies stage shootings, it means that America's gun violence is not real and has been manufactured in order to disarm the populace.

Further Reading: Yglesias, Matthew (February 22, 2018) The Parkland conspiracy theories, explained.

Area 51

In 1947, claims that an "alien spacecraft" landed in Roswell, New Mexico, were dismissed by the U.S. military, which said the object was merely a weather balloon. Theorists believe the craft was taken into Area 51, a secret Air Force military installation located at Groom Lake in southern Nevada, not accessible to the public and under 24-hour surveillance. In 1989 a man named Robert ("Bob") Lazar worked on extraterrestrial technology inside Area 51. Lazar claimed he saw autopsy photographs of aliens inside the facility and that the government used the facility to examine recovered alien spacecraft and reverse-engineer the highly advanced technology. He insisted that he has no idea how the government got their hands on the alien craft, and that his life had been threatened over this information. Details of Area 51 are classified for purposes of national security — providing further proof that the military is hiding aliens or alien spacecraft. It is not known why Area 51 is called "Area 51."

Further Reading: Knox, Patrick (July 2, 2018) Where is Area 51, how is it connected to aliens and what are the Roswell UFO conspiracy theories? <www.thesun.co.uk>

Nazca Mummies

Nazca is a city and system of valleys on the southern coast of Peru. Since their first discovery eighty years ago, a group of very large trenches in the Nazca Desert have fascinated people from around the world, sparking speculation over whether the ancient Nazca people carved out the giant designs for irrigation, signaling aliens, or as offerings to the gods. These "Nazca Lines" consist of roughly 800 straight lines which stretch up to 30 miles, 300 geometric shapes which include triangles, rectangles, spirals, and arrows, and 80 animal and plant designs, including a spider, a cactus, and one dubbed "The Astronaut," which looks like a human figure wearing a space helmet. In 2017, six fifth-century mummies unearthed in Nazca were found to have different anatomical structure to humans. Researchers from St. Petersburg believe the three-fingered mummies with elongated heads could be representatives of an alien race which had possibly reached a stage of advancement much earlier than Earthlings.

Further Reading: Williams, Sophie (March 13, 2018) Three-fingered Peruvian mummies unearthed in tomb last year "have alien anatomy." <www.standard.co.uk>

ʻOumuamua

Astronomers first suspected that a cigar-shaped object 2,600 feet (800 meters) long and 260 feet (80 meters) wide spotted hurtling through the solar system was an interstellar asteroid, however, its curious shape led them to propose sweeping it for radio signals in case it happened to be an alien craft or an artificial light sail. ʻOumuamua, meaning "messenger" or "scout" in Hawaiian, was first seen in October 2017 by the Pan-STARRS 1 telescope in Hawaii. More recently, astrophysicist Marco Micheli discovered that the long, slender object was not moving as it should. Instead, it shows a "really strong non-gravitational acceleration," which means its motion indicates that gravity is not the only thing dictating its path. Also unusual, no dust is seen coming from the object. When gas escapes from a comet, it generally carries surface dust with it, and the stronger the outgassing, the larger the grains of dust it can liberate. These strange properties have prompted some to suspect alien-built origin.

Further Reading: Klesman, Alison (November 8, 2018) What do we know about Oumuamua?

Reptilians

According to research by New Age philosopher David Icke, a race of Reptilian aliens are here on Earth to crossbreed with select, unsuspecting humans in order to create desired "elite" bloodlines that will eventually be used to control the world. He cites references throughout history regarding worship of reptile gods and other entities, such as the Aztec serpent god Quetzalcoatl and Naga of India as evidence of contact with Reptilian masters. He suggests that Reptilians spread their bloodline through generations of royal families, owners of the world's banks, and heads of the biggest worldwide corporations, and he claims the bloodline includes 43 American presidents, three British and two Canadian prime ministers, the Rockefellers, Rothschilds, various European aristocratic families, the establishment families of the Eastern United States, and the British House of Windsor. He predicts that Reptilians will eventually spend more time among us and keep occupying more positions of power until the human race bends completely to their control.

Further Reading: Reyes, Scarlett (June 4, 2018) 10 Shocking Facts About The Reptilian Conspiracy.

Project MK-Ultra

The Central Intelligence Agency has been involved in developing sophisticated mind control programs since the early 1950s. Project MK-Ultra is the most infamous of these, conducted on hundreds of unwitting U.S. citizens. The CIA used numerous methodologies to manipulate people's mental states and alter brain functions, including the surreptitious administration of LSD and other chemicals, hypnosis, sensory deprivation, isolation, verbal and sexual abuse, as well as various forms of torture for mind control, information gathering and psychological torture. Many of the tests were conducted at universities, hospitals or prisons in the United States and Canada. Most took place between 1953 and 1964, but it's not clear how many people were involved in the tests since the agency kept notoriously poor records and destroyed most MK-Ultra documents. Although the program was terminated in the late 1960s, it is believed that other even more sophisticated top secret mind control programs continue to this day.

Further Reading: Eschner, Kat (April 13, 2017) What We Know About the CIA's Midcentury Mind-Control Project. <www.smithsonianmag.com>

Tavistock Institute

The Tavistock Institute, founded in London in 1946 with the aid of a grant from the Rockefeller Foundation, describes itself as a nonprofit charity that applies social science to contemporary issues and problems. But with its connections to U.S. research institutes, think tanks, and the drug industry, the Tavistock grew from a somewhat crude beginning into a sophisticated organization that intends to shape the destiny of the entire planet and change the paradigm of modern society. The Institute developed mass brainwashing techniques first used experimentally on American prisoners of war in Korea. Its experiments in social engineering activities have been widely used on the American public, modifying individual behavior through topical psychology. Researchers design incidents that leave people afraid, concerned and worried, study the results and work to change their psychological and neurologic states. When worry becomes a part of society, it becomes much easier to manipulate the masses.

Further Reading: Estulin, Daniel (September 14, 2015) Tavistock Institute: Social Engineering the Masses. <www. postflaviana.org>

The Illuminati

The secret society was started in 1776 in Bavaria by Adam Weishaupt, a professor of canon law at the University of Ingolstadt. He intended to illuminate, enlighten, and perfect human nature through re-education to achieve a communal state with nature, free of government and organized religion. The Illuminati was stamped out by a government crackdown on secret societies in the late 1780s, but many believe that it has continued to survive as an underground organization connected with the New World Order, a current political idea about a one-world government, religion, and financial system with centralization making it easier to control the masses. Organizations such as the United Nations, the International Monetary Fund, and the World Bank are seen as tentacles of the Illuminati, intending to create and then manage crises that will eventually convince the masses that globalism is the necessary solution to the world's woes. The symbol most associated with the Illuminati is the pyramid-and-eye symbol adorning the $1 bill.

Further Reading: Edwards, Phil (January 18, 2016) 9 questions about the Illuminati you were too afraid to ask. <www.vox.com>

George Soros

Born in Hungary in 1930, George Soros lived through the Nazi occupation and the murder of over 500,000 Hungarian Jews. In 1947, as the Communists took power, Soros left Budapest for London, then migrated to the United States, entering the world of finance and investments where he amassed a fortune as one of the world's greatest speculators in the global financial markets. Soros has become a "puppet master," pulling the strings behind global political developments and granting money to liberal organizations around the world to advance the Soros vision of how the world ought to be. Through his main group, the Open Society Foundations, a network of foundations, partners, and projects in more than 100 countries, he has provided $18 billion to radical infiltrators who have been quietly transforming societal, cultural, and political institutions for more than a generation. Soros is the mastermind of a "globalist" movement, shaping the world into one global society without borders or individual governments.

Further Reading: Goudsmit, Linda (November 6, 2017) The Humanitarian Hoax of George Soros.

Nibiru Cataclysm

The International Astronomical Union's Minor Planet Center, a group of scientists led by the Carnegie Institution for Science, has confirmed the discovery of an object at the edge of the solar system that hints at the existence of an even-farther-away object that could be the elusive Niburu or Planet X, a "Super-Earth" that could have a mass up to 10 times that of our planet. Mainstream astronomers have long speculated about the existence of an unknown planet at a distance of more than 2 trillion miles, far beyond the orbit of Pluto that would account for the anomalies they have detected in the orbits of Neptune and Uranus. Some unseen body seems to be tugging at them. There have been many warnings about the approach of Nibiru, as the gravitational pull of a planet entering the inner solar system would have profound effects on the other orbiting bodies, including Earth, causing floods, earthquakes, volcanic eruptions, a pole shift, and perhaps stop the Earth's rotation for three days, citing the "three days of darkness" predicted in the Bible.

Further Reading: Hamill, Jasper (April 13, 2018) What would happen if the apocalypse death planet Nibiru smashed into Earth? <www.metro.co.uk>

Common Purpose

In the autumn of 1988, Julia Mary Middleton formed Common Purpose in the UK, on the surface an educational charity that runs a range of development courses to train leaders of the future, when, in fact, it has been described as an Orwellian engine of social takeover, a corrupt, subversive, secretive and deeply sinister organization with a hidden agenda to promote communitarian corporate-communism and a European super-state. The true objectives of Common Purpose are social control in a collectivist and corporatist society, the destruction of the national identity of Great Britain, the destruction of democracy, the undermining of traditional beliefs and values, and the secretive merging of the public and private sectors into a state-controlled partnership. The current state of economic and social chaos has been deliberately engineered by Common Purpose along with New World Order plotters, their work funded by public money and big business, including international banks and financial cabals.

Further Reading: Everiss, Bruce (August 11, 2017) Common Purpose is Sinister and Evil. The Proof. Retrieved from <www.bruceonpolitics.com>

Skull and Bones Society

A secret, semi-occult society at Yale University, Skull and Bones has become a cultural institution known for its powerful alumni and sinister conspiracy theories since its founding in 1832. Throughout history, some of the most prominent American figures have been Bonesmen, handpicked members of Yale's undergraduate class, selected to join the ranks of elite students. Bonesmen have had control over the fortunes of the Rockefellers, the Carnegies, and the Fords. Members have, at one time, controlled the fortunes of the Carnegie, Rockefeller and Ford families, as well as posts in the Central Intelligence Agency, the American Psychological Association, the Council on Foreign Relations and some of the most powerful law firms in the world. Theorists believe that the clandestine group was created as a way to build a modern Illuminati, and they reportedly hatch schemes of world domination at the "Tomb," an imposing, windowless crypt in New Haven, Connecticut.

Further Reading: Serena, Katie (November 22, 2017) The Secret History of The Skull and Bones Society – and The Powerful Men Behind It. Retrieved from <www.allthatsinteresting.com>

Young Earth

A new generation of Christian scholars and scientists, armed with earned doctorates and a literal view of the Genesis Creation narrative, has breathed new life into the theory that the Earth is thousands, not billions, of years old. The Young Earth belief, based on a particular literal interpretation of Genesis 1-11 in the Hebrew Bible, holds that the universe is only 6,000 to 10,000 years old and was created over a period of six ordinary (solar/24-hour) days, with God then "resting" on the seventh day. They regard the Bible as a historically accurate, factually inerrant record of natural history. Proponents also believe that all living things, including humans, were created in a very short period of time in essentially the forms in which they exist today, as a part of the movement's rejection of evolution. They believe that 2,300 to 3,300 years before Christ, the surface of the earth was radically rearranged by Noah's Flood. They further argue that scientific evidence is consistent with the creationary point of view.

Further Reading: Hovind, Eric (May 6, 2010) Evidence for a Young Earth. <www.creationtoday.org>

Moon Landings

The United States and former Soviet Union were in a "space race" to get to the moon first, supposedly to show the superiority of their socioeconomic systems. Theorists claim that the U.S. government, desperate to beat the Russians, faked the lunar landings, with Neil Armstrong and Buzz Aldrin acting out their mission on a secret film set, with advanced special effects developed by Stanley Kubrick for his 1968 sci-fi masterpiece *2001: A Space Odyssey*. It has been claimed that when 2001 was in post-production, NASA secretly approached Kubrick to direct the first three moon landings. The launch and splashdown were real but the spacecraft stayed in Earth orbit and faked footage broadcast as "live from the Moon." Critics point to the lack of stars in the lunar sky, shadows falling in multiple directions and the presence of a "prop rock" labelled with a "C." But the most conclusive evidence they believe can be found in the footage of Aldrin planting a fluttering American flag on the moon's surface, impossible in the vacuum of the lunar surface.

Further Reading: Black, Joanne (October 13, 2018) The myths and legends of the moon landing. Retrieved from <www.noted.co.nz>

AIDS

Since the Centers for Disease Control and Prevention first reported the HIV/AIDS epidemic in 1981, rumors have persisted that the deadly virus was created by the CIA to wipe out homosexuals and African-Americans. South African President Thabo Mbeki has disputed scientific claims that the virus originated in Africa and accused the U.S. government of manufacturing the disease in military labs. When she won the Nobel Peace Prize, Kenyan ecologist Wangari Maathai used the international spotlight to support the same theory. Some insist that the government deliberately injected gay men with the virus during 1978 hepatitis-B experiments. Still others point to scientists at the Cold Spring Harbor lab in New York who they believe engineered HIV, and that the World Health Organization spread the virus under cover of the smallpox eradication program. The Rev. Jerry Falwell famously argued that AIDS is a plague sent by God to punish homosexuals and American society for tolerating homosexuality.

Further Reading: Lapidos, Juliet (March 19, 2008) The AIDS Conspiracy Handbook. <www.slate.com>

The Holocaust

While historians differ on the exact number of Jews killed at the hands of the Nazis, the most commonly cited figure for the total number has been six million. That number was first been mentioned by Dr. Wilhelm Hoettl, an Austrian Nazi Party member, SS member, and a trained historian who served in a number of senior positions in the Third Reich. In November 1945, Hoettl testified for the prosecution in the Nuremberg trials of accused Nazi war criminals. "Holocaust deniers" claim that the figure of six million Jewish deaths is an exaggeration and that deaths in the concentration camps were the results of typhus or legitimate executions by the Nazi state for actual criminal offenses. They assert that Jews and the Allied powers deliberately inflated the numbers of Jews killed during the war. Rabbi Yosef Mizrachi, based in New York, has said that fewer than one million Jews were killed in the Holocaust, claiming most of those counted among the usually cited figure of six million were not Jewish according to rabbinical law.

Further Reading: Stuart, Hunter (April 25, 2017) People Still Think the Holocaust Was a Hoax. <www.medium.com>

The Rothschilds

The Rothschild family, the most famous of all European banking dynasties, has for 200 years exerted great influence on the economic and, indirectly, the political history of Europe. Starting out in a Frankfurt banking house, Mayer Amschel Rothschild and his sons became international bankers, establishing branches in London, Paris, Vienna, and Naples by the 1820s. The Rothschilds became successful by lending money to the various governments of Europe who needed to fund their unending wars with one another. They have supplied capital to both the winners and losers of all wars since the early 19th century — whichever side won, they profited. They have used their money and power to influence the economies of several countries, creating economic crashes to profit from them. With a current net worth estimated at up to $700 trillion, the family continues to consolidate power until a New World Order is established with the Rothschilds as central players with complete domination of the world's resources.

Further Reading: Dunning, Brian (May 22, 2012) Deconstructing the Rothschild Conspiracy. <www.skeptoid.com>

September 11, 2001

America was shaken to its core when planes were flown into the twin towers of the World Trade Center in New York and the Pentagon in Washington, D.C. on September 11, 2001, killing nearly 3,000 people. Al-Qaeda took responsibility for the attacks, which was confirmed by U.S. intelligence, but many suspect the attacks were an inside job, with the government orchestrating the events of that day in order to justify subsequent wars in the Middle East. Critics assert that the towers were brought down in what appeared to be a controlled demolition with explosives placed in selected locations. Some witnesses recounted hearing explosions inside the building as they attempted to escape. Many architects and scientists maintain that a plane's fuel cannot produce enough heat to melt the steel frames of the two buildings that collapsed. Commercial airplane frames are constructed with a very light aluminum material in order to make it easier to fly, and theorists maintain there is no possible way airplanes can do as much damage to the Twin Towers as reported.

Further Reading: Gaia Staff (September 11, 2017) Was 9/11 a False Flag? WTC 7 Might Be the Smoking Gun. <www.gaia.com>

Solar Warden

There are claims of a secret space program, including a fleet of human spaceships charged with monitoring alien traffic throughout our solar system and perhaps planning to defend our solar system in the event of an extraterrestrial attack. Solar Warden is the code name for this secret space fleet, in operation since 1980 under U.S. Air Force Command. It is said that there are approximately eight cigar-shaped motherships (each longer than two football fields end-to-end) and 43 small craft called "scout ships." There are suspected to be least 300 personnel involved at these facilities, aerospace Black Project contractors with some contributions of parts and systems by Canada, the United Kingdom, Italy, Austria, Russia, and Australia. If Solar Warden is indeed real, it would require advanced technology several generations ahead of what our military currently uses on the battlefield. Some speculate that reverse-engineered alien technology is responsible for the rapid development of these types of systems.

Further Reading: Darin, Paul (February 17, 2015) The Solar Warden Covert Space Project: Fact or Science Fiction? <www.theepochtimes.com>

Montauk Project

A series of secret United States government projects were allegedly conducted in the early 1980s at Camp Hero State Park, located at the far eastern tip of Long Island, for the purpose of developing psychological warfare techniques and exotic government/military experiments in fields such as time travel, teleportation, mind control, a continuation of the 1943 Philadelphia Experiment which opened up a wormhole and rendered the USS Eldridge battleship "cloaked" to enemy devices. The first test resulted in the Eldridge being rendered nearly invisible, with some witnesses reporting a greenish fog appearing in its place. The experiment was repeated on October 28, 1943. This time, Eldridge not only became invisible, but she disappeared from the area in a flash of blue light and teleported to Norfolk, Virginia, over 200 miles away. The Netflix TV series *Stranger Things* was allegedly inspired by the Montauk Project, and at one time Montauk was used as its working title.

Further Reading: Schneider, Jason (October 30, 2018) "Stranger Things" in the Hamptons: The Story of the Montauk Project. <www.outeast.com>

Tectonic Weapons

A tectonic weapon is a hypothetical device or system which functions by creating a powerful charge of elastic energy in the Earth's crust. It then becomes an earthquake once triggered by a nuclear explosion in the epicenter or a vast electric pulse. An unconfirmed report by the Russian Northern Fleet suggests that the devastating Haiti earthquake in 2010 was caused by a U.S. Navy earthquake weapons test that went horribly wrong, killing more than 100,000 people. The weapon was being tested for possible use against Iran, according to the Russian report, in order to topple the Islamic system in the country. A similar Russian weapon allegedly caused an earthquake on Georgian territory several years ago. In 1997, former US Secretary of Defense William Cohen expressed concern over countries engaging in "eco-type of terrorism whereby they can alter the climate, set off earthquakes, volcanoes remotely through the use of electromagnetic waves."

Further Reading: Dmitry, Baxter (June 13, 2016) US Military Create California Earthquake Using Seismic Weapon. <www.newspunch.com>

Codex Alimentarius

The Codex Alimentarius Commission, a Rome-based organization, was established in 1961 by the United Nations with the stated aim of being a "global reference point for consumers, food producers and processors, national food control agencies and the international food trade." But under the guise of protecting public safety through standardization of food, nutrient, and botanical codes, the commission is regarded by many as a means for the pharmaceutical industry to eventually make all supplements available by prescription only. These rules were originally proposed by a German Codex delegation sponsored by three drug companies: Hoechst, Bayer, and BASF. And, in fact, elements of Codex proposals already exist as law in Germany and Norway. In Germany, a number of high-potency agents are available only through pharmacists, and as a result, a vast number of natural agents are either not available or available only by prescription, at great cost. Codex Alimentarius is Latin for "food and nutrition code."

Further Reading: Mead, Nathaniel (September/October 1998) The Codex Conspiracy. <www.utne.com>

North American Union

A theoretical economic and political continental union of Canada, Mexico, and the United States has been the subject of academic theory for over a century. Since 2005, claims have emerged that a North American Union, loosely based on the European Union, was not only being planned, but was being implemented by the three governments. Critics have cited the formation of the Security and Prosperity Partnership of North America, claiming it was an attempt to dramatically alter the economic and political status quo between the countries outside the scrutiny of the respective national legislatures. Conservative activists are convinced that the SPP is the first step in a secret plan to dissolve the three nations into one continental unit. Theorists believe that goods and people will flow among the three countries unimpeded, aided by a network of continent-girdling superhighways. The U.S. and Canadian dollars, along with the peso, will be phased out and replaced by a common North American currency called the "amero."

Further Reading: Russell, John (July 8, 2018) The Amero Conspiracy. <www.thebalance.com>

The Titanic

Late in the evening on April 14, 1912, the R.M.S. Titanic hit an iceberg and sank into the icy waters of the North Atlantic, killing 1,517 of the 2,223 passengers and crew members aboard. In 1910, at a clandestine meeting hosted by J. P. Morgan, seven major financiers came to an agreement on the need to create a central bank backed by the United States Government, to be known later as the Federal Reserve. This scheme, however, was opposed by certain influential businessmen such as Benjamin Guggenheim, Isidor Straus and John Jacob Astor IV. In order to eliminate these three powerful "enemies," Morgan arranged for them to board the Titanic for a pre-arranged fatal maiden voyage. The ship's captain, Edward Smith, was ordered to run his ship at full speed through an ice field on a moonless night, ignoring any ice warnings including those from the lookouts, with the purpose of hitting an iceberg severely enough to cause the ship to founder and the three businessmen to drown. After the sinking, all opposition to the Federal Reserve disappeared.

Further Reading: Adl-Tabatabai (October 31, 2017) New Evidence Reveals JP Morgan Sunk Titanic to Form Federal Reserve. <www.newspunch.com>

Coca-Cola

In April of 1985, Coca-Cola launched a reformulated version of its flagship soft drink they called New Coke. Consumer reaction to the change was negative, and New Coke was a colossal marketing blunder. The company reintroduced Coke's original formula within three months of New Coke's debut, rebranded as Coca-Cola Classic, but that's not the whole story. The world's best-selling soft drink once contained cocaine, and even after the addictive stimulant was removed, the formula included a non-narcotic extract from coca, the plant from which cocaine is derived. The 1985 reformulation provided cover for the final removal of all coca derivatives from the product to placate the Drug Enforcement Administration, which was trying to eradicate the plant worldwide in order to combat an increase in cocaine trafficking and consumption. Environmental historian Bartow Elmore, author of *Citizen Coke*, confirmed the reformulation was made in response to the escalating War on Drugs by the Reagan Administration.

Further Reading: Vigliotti, Jake. The untold truth of Coke. <www.mashed.com/44149/secrets-coca-cola-doesnt-want-know>

AI Takeover

Robot rebellions have been a major theme throughout science fiction for many decades. In 2014, theoretical physicist Stephen Hawking said that "Success in creating Artificial Intelligence would be the biggest event in human history. Unfortunately, it might also be the last, unless we learn how to avoid the risks." Hawking believed that in the coming decades, AI could offer "incalculable benefits and risks" such as "technology outsmarting financial markets, out-inventing human researchers, and developing weapons we cannot even understand." He suggested a hypothetical scenario in which AI becomes the dominant form of intelligence on Earth and expressed concerns about the possibility that AI could develop to the point that humans could not control it, theorizing that this could "spell the end of the human race." Other scientists point to the possibility of humans upgrading their capabilities with bionics and/or genetic engineering and, as cyborgs, becoming the dominant species in themselves.

Further Reading: Ozoalor, Dave Partner ((November 17, 2017) Blockchains: The AI that will take over the world has already been born! <www.becominghuman.ai>

Sovereign Citizens

The Sovereign Citizens Movement originated in 1971 with the teachings of Col. William P. Gale, a leading figure in the anti-tax and paramilitary movements. Sovereign Citizens believe that the American legal system originally set up by the founding fathers, or common law, was secretly replaced by a new government system based on admiralty law, the law of the sea, and international commerce. Under common law, they believe, Sovereigns would be free men, but under admiralty law, they are slaves, and secret government forces have a vested interest in keeping them that way. Some Sovereigns believe this treasonous change occurred during the Civil War, while others blame the events of 1933 when the U.S. abandoned the gold standard. Sovereigns claim that they ——not judges, juries, law enforcement or elected officials — get to decide which laws to obey and which to ignore, and they don't think they should have to pay taxes. The Federal Bureau of Investigation classifies some Sovereign Citizens as domestic terrorists.

Further Reading: Goode, Erica (August 23, 2013) In Paper War, Flood of Liens Is the Weapon.

Princess Diana

She was the first wife of Charles, Prince of Wales, heir apparent to the British throne, and at one time the world's most photographed woman. On August 31, 1997, while being pursued by paparazzi, the car carrying Princess Diana and boyfriend Dodi Fayed crashed inside the Alma Tunnel in Paris. Almost immediately, rumors began to surface that a royal conspiracy was behind the fatal car crash. The official French inquiry, conducted in near-total secrecy, concluded that the couple's driver, Henri Paul, who was also killed, was at fault for the crash. According to reports, Paul was impaired by drugs and alcohol and was driving at nearly twice the speed limit when he lost control of the car in a Paris tunnel. But Fayed's father, Egyptian businessman Mohamed Al Fayed, claimed the romance was an embarrassment to the royal family, and that her death was the result of a scheme involving Prince Phillip, Prince Charles and the CIA. Al Fayed also stated that Diana was pregnant with Dodi Fayed's child at the time of her death.

Further Reading: Griffin, Andrew (August 31, 2017) Princess Diana conspiracy theories: Eight reasons people believe the crash in Paris wasn't all it seems.

Water Fluoridation

The addition of fluoride to the water supply for the purpose of preventing tooth decay began in the 1940s. For many years we were told that fluoride needed to be swallowed to be effective, but more recent research has since shown that fluoride's benefit comes primarily from topical application, not ingestion. There was never any need, therefore, to swallow fluoridated water. Opponents of water fluoridation view it as an infringement of individual rights, if not an outright violation of medical ethics, on the basis that individuals have no choice in the water that they drink. Antifluoridation literature links fluoride exposure to a wide variety of effects, including AIDS, allergy, Alzheimer's disease, arthritis, cancer, and low IQ, along with diseases of the gastrointestinal tract, kidney, pineal gland, and thyroid. The opposition also points to osteosarcoma, an extremely rare bone cancer linked to fluoride, which collects over time in bones. Right-wing groups like the John Birch Society have long implied dark motives behind fluoridation.

Further Reading: Ewens, Av Hannah (August 11, 2016) A Deep Dive Into the Conspiracy Theory That Governments Are Controlling Us with Fluoride. <www.vice.com>

Daylight Savings Time

Daylight Savings Time is the practice of setting the clocks forward one hour from standard time during the summer months, and back again in the fall, in order to make better use of natural daylight. But the idea of maximizing daylight is actually an archaic practice first thought up in the late 1700s and often attributed to Benjamin Franklin as a way to accommodate agricultural workers and farmers. A more recent push for Daylight Savings Time suggests that it helps conserve energy, but as technology advanced, those savings disappeared. Some studies have shown that the time change has led to fewer road accidents and injuries by supplying more daylight during the hours more people use the roads, but Carnegie Mellon research that found people walking near traffic during rush hour in the first few weeks after Daylight Savings Time ends were more likely to be fatally struck by cars than before the change. A Swedish study found that the risk of having a heart attack increases in the first 3 weekdays after switching to DST in the spring.

Further Reading: Abad-Santos, Alexander (November 1, 2013) Daylight Saving Time Is America's Greatest Shame. <www.the atlantic.com>

Chronovisor

A device called the chronovisor was allegedly a functional time viewer built by Pellegrino Ernetti, an Italian priest and scientist. Described as a large cabinet with a cathode ray tube for viewing the received events and a series of buttons, levers, and other controls for selecting the time and the location to be viewed, the chronovisor could also locate and track specific individuals. According to its inventor, the device worked by receiving, decoding and reproducing the electromagnetic radiation left behind from past events. It could also pick up the audio component or sound waves emitted by these same events. Father Ernetti asserted that, using the chronovisor as his eyes and ears, he had witnessed Christ dying on the cross, a speech given by Napoleon Bonaparte, and the destruction of Sodom and Gomorrah. Before Father Ernetti died in April 1994, he wrote a letter in which he insisted that the device was real and was not a hoax as many believed. The device has long been rumored to still exist somewhere in the Vatican.

Further Reading: Lowth, Marcus (January 18, 2019) The Chronovisor – The Vatican's Secret "Time-Seeing" Device? <www.ufoinsight.com>

Benghazi

On September 11, 2012, an attack on the American consulate in Benghazi, Libya ended in the death of four Americans: Sean Smith, Glen Doherty, and Tyrone Woods; and U.S. Ambassador John Christopher Stevens. Initially, the deaths were blamed on a spontaneous protest, but it was later determined that the strike was a premeditated terrorist attack. Secretary of State Hillary Clinton did not take heed of intelligence warnings before the attack. Her State Department refused to call in available military support during the attack, and after the attack it took steps to cover up what had happened. Some allege that the Obama administration arranged the attack for political reasons, and Senator Rand Paul has asserted that the government's response to the incident was designed to distract from a secret CIA operation. Ahmed Abu Khattala, ringleader of the attack, was convicted of providing material support to terrorists and using a semiautomatic weapon during a violent crime. He was acquitted of murder and other charges.

Further Reading: Read, Max (May 10, 2013) What the Fuck Is All This Benghazi Shit: An Explainer.

Protocols of Zion

Originating in Russia in the early 1900s, *The Protocols of the Learned Elders of Zion* is a document that purports to reveal the secret plans of a Jewish cabal to undermine the health, family life, and morality of non-Jews. The book, which contains strange-looking symbols, is said to be the meeting notes from a clandestine gathering of Jewish leaders, "The Elders of Zion," who outlined their plan to slowly take over the world's media, governments and banks in an effort to destroy Christianity, replacing traditional social order with one based on mass manipulation. The authenticity of *The Protocols* has been challenged in public trials, and scholars have suggested that it was fabricated by the Russian Okhrana, or Czarist secret police, however the document has remained a staple of anti-Semitic ideology throughout the world and served to rationalize genocide in Hitler's Germany. The document has proved remarkably resilient and has become a major source of Arab and Islamic propaganda.

Further Reading: Brivati, Brian (April 24, 2006) The enduring attraction of the Protocols of Zion.
www.theguardian.com

Colony Collapse Disorder

Worldwide honeybee colonies have been disappearing for the past few years. Between 50% and 90% of hives have been destroyed since 2004. Since bees pollinate at least 19 kinds of fruits, vegetables and nuts, the downstream effects of their disappearance could be devastating. In the phenomenon known as Colony Collapse Disorder, bees in an infected hive leave and never return. The colony dwindles down until it cannot sustain itself and dies. Research continues to find that a class of pesticides called neonicotinoids are killing off the world's bee population. After the initial news release containing the damning information on pesticide contamination, another release came out of the Associated Press. Conspicuous by its absence was any mention of pesticide contamination at all, with "unknown causes" listed as the reason for the bee die-offs. Monsanto, a company that dominates America's food chain with ruthless tactics, responded to the first news release with enough clout to have the pesticide cause removed from consideration.

Further Reading: Frej, Willa (February 26, 2016) Bees Are Dying And That Could Be Devastating For Food Security. <www.huffingtonpost.com>

RFID Chips

An advanced identification process in which an individual or item is tagged with a specific ID number, RFID (Radio Frequency Identification) uses radio waves that a computerized reader can scan to access stored information. Active tags have a local power source and may operate hundreds of meters from the RFID reader. The device, which is inserted through the skin in a procedure that takes less than 10 minutes, is no bigger than a grain of rice. This technology causes uneasiness for many, particularly with recent concerns over privacy violations and the improper handling of sensitive data. If someone can read it, then there is always someone who can hack into it. For historians it sparks thoughts of George Orwell's *1984* and evangelical Christians it represents the biblical "Mark of the Beast" described in the book of Revelation. Without it no one will be able to buy or sell, Revelation 13:16-17. The Bible warns Christians not to take this mark or face eternal consequences as described in Revelation 14:9-10.

Further Reading: Palmer, Shelly (August 28, 2017) Chipping People: Are You Ready? www.adage.com

Phoebus Cartel

In 1924, leaders of the lighting industry, Osram, Philips, and General Electric, created "Phoebus, Inc.," a cartel whose sole purpose was control of the manufacture and sale of all electric lightbulbs. It was one of the first organizations that introduced planned obsolescence — a policy of planning or designing a product with an artificially limited lifespan. Motivated by profits, the cartel took its business of shortening the lifetime of bulbs as seriously as earlier researchers had approached their job of lengthening it. What ultimately killed Phoebus, however, was World War II. As the members countries went to war, close coordination became impossible, and although the cartel's 1924 agreement was supposed to last until 1955, it was nullified in 1940. In 1975, German clockmaker Dieter Binninger invented a light bulb with a guaranteed lifetime of 150,000 hours (approximately 17 years). Unfortunately, Binninger died in a suspicious plane crash, and his light bulb patent disappeared immediately after his death.

Further Reading: Krajewski, Markus (September 24, 2017) The Great Lightbulb Conspiracy.

Tupac Shakur

One of hip-hop's most iconic figures, Tupac Shakur was in Las Vegas on September 7, 1996, for the Mike Tyson-Bruce Seldon heavyweight championship fight, where he and others in his entourage were captured on tape in the lobby of the MGM Grand hotel engaging in a scuffle with a member of the Los Angeles-based Bloods street gang. Hours later, Shakur was a passenger in a car driven by Death Row Records head Marian "Suge" Knight when a white Cadillac pulled up alongside them at a stoplight and opened fire. At least 12 shots were fired, four of which struck Shakur. Emergency surgery at University Medical Center saved Shakur's life, and in the days following, doctors announced that his chances of recovery had improved. However, on September 13, 1996, Tupac Shakur supposedly died of his wounds. Theorists assert that his death was faked, most likely by Tupac himself, and that he's still alive in hiding. Tupac has been sighted in New York, New Jersey, Los Angeles, Malaysia, Somalia, Cuba, and Sweden.

Further Reading: Akingbade, Tobi (October 5, 2018) Tupac alive? Everywhere the late rapper has been 'spotted' as conspiracy theories resurface. <www.metro.co.uk>

Hubbert's Peak

In 1956, geologist and geophysicist Marion King Hubbert presented a paper indicating that any finite resource must have a beginning, middle and end of production and must reach a point of maximum output followed by a decline, and he predicted that petroleum would one day reach its peak in terms of production. During his research Hubbert was working for the Shell Oil company, and many suspected that his theory of peak oil was fabricated by a group of oil producers to create a state of artificial scarcity and push up the price of crude. Russian geologist, Nikolai Kudryavtsev believed the idea that oil formed through a process taking millions of years from the remains of dinosaurs and ancient plants was wrong. Instead, he believed oil production was a much faster process, something that is happening constantly within the Earth. Essentially, oil is a sustainable material and the extraordinary rise and fall of prices confirms that there is constant manipulation of the availability of oil on the market.

Further Reading: Lowth, Marcus (July 29, 2018) The Peak Oil Conspiracy, The Petrodollar, And What It Means Today. <www.ufoinsight.com>

Atlantis

The legend of Atlantis first appears in western literature in the works of Plato. In a story the Greek philosopher attributes to Egyptians, the gods destroyed Atlantis in a single day and night by earthquakes and floods and sunk it into the sea. About 3,600 years ago, a highly advanced society of Minoans lived on Santorini, an island in the Aegean Sea near Greece. The Minoan civilization was notable for its large and elaborate palaces, some of which were up to four stories high, featuring complex plumbing systems that were unheard of in the ancient world. The advanced shipbuilding of the Minoans is claimed to have been unmatched until the 1950s. With a catastrophic volcanic eruption, in fact one of the largest volcanic events on Earth in recorded history, the Minoan civilization suddenly disappeared. It is speculated that Plato borrowed from stories of the Minoan civilization and incorporated them into his account of the lost island continent. It is likely that the Minoan eruption of Santorini and the destruction of Atlantis are the same event.

Further Reading: Zhang, Sarah (August 9, 2018) The Mystery of the Ancient Volcano That May Have Inspired Atlantis. <www.theatlantic.com>

Freemasonry

George Washington, Benjamin Franklin, Paul Revere and other iconic Americans were members of the Freemasons, a secretive fraternity of powerful men established in the Middle Ages and carried on today. Nine Freemasons signed the Declaration of Independence and historians note that the Constitution and the Bill of Rights both seem to be heavily influenced by the Masonic "civil religion" which focuses on freedom, free enterprise, and a limited role for the state. Theorists allege that Freemasons have slipped their secret symbols into American icons. An aerial view of Washington D. C. shows that the Capitol building, Washington Monument, Lincoln Memorial and White House form a plane. On that plane, the Capitol building, Jefferson Memorial, and White house form the Freemason compass. Freemasons claim to be a fraternal group of men seeking only self-improvement and the betterment of society, but they have long been suspected of occult worship and shadow manipulation.

Further Reading: Westmaas, Reuben (August 3,2018) The Freemasons Are a Real Secret Society that Dates Back to The 1600s. <www.curiosity.com>

Vaccines

A popular conspiracy theory states that the pharmaceutical industry has mounted a cover-up of a causal link between vaccines and autism. The theory took hold in 1998 with the publication of a study that suggested the MMR (measles-mumps-rubella) vaccine, or infection with the naturally occurring measles virus itself, might cause autism. Rates of autism in developing countries have risen remarkably in the past 20 years. For children born in 1992, according to the U.S. CDC, about 1 in 150 were diagnosed with an autism spectrum disorder (ASD). For children born in 2004, about 1 in 68 children received an ASD diagnosis. Researchers and worried parents have speculated about causes of autism, and the issue has been widely studied. The role of vaccines has been questioned, along with other possible risk factors for ASD, such as genetic predisposition, advanced parental age, and other environmental factors. Skeptical of modern medicine, anti-vaxxers believe that vaccination is part of a conspiracy to lower the population.

Further Reading: Micozzi, Marc (February 16, 2015) The hidden, ugly truth about vaccines. <www.drmicozzi.com>

The Holy Grail

According to legend, Mary Magdalene used a stone cup to collect a few drops of Christ's blood during the Crucifixion, thus bestowing it with sacred power. Those who drank from the cup, it was said, could be cured of all ills, and even attain immortality. Thomas Wright, a 19th-century writer and historian, claimed the cup was seized from the Temple Mount in Jerusalem by the Knights Templar during the Crusades and smuggled to Britain where it was entrusted to Payne Peveril. His family became the Grail Keepers, and sometime in the mid-19th century a Perevel descendent transferred the legendary relic from Whittington Castle, Shropshire in the West Midlands, to Alberbury Priory, then to a hiding place inside a statue of St. John that stood in Hawkstone Park. The small egg cup-shaped vessel made from green alabaster (the material as described in the Bible) was discovered there in 1934, dated by archaeologists and historians at the British Museum to the First Century AD.

Further Reading: Phillips, Graham (January 19, 2017) The Chalice of Magdalene – Is this the Holy Grail?
<www.ancient-origins.net>

Trilateral Commission

A policy-oriented forum founded by David Rockefeller in July 1973, the Trilateral Commission includes members from the worlds of business, government, academia, press and media tasked with fostering closer cooperation among core industrialized areas of the world. They have proposed the removal of key parts of monetary, fiscal and trade policy from the direct control of the public and instead placed in the hands of more distant bodies, namely international organizations and "independent" bodies separate from governments. Many believe this group of international elites controls the wheels of governments, industries, and media organizations, with the real goal of establishing global hegemony. Republican Senator Barry Goldwater suggested the group was "a skillful, coordinated effort to seize control and consolidate the four centers of power: political, monetary, intellectual, and ecclesiastical in the creation of a worldwide economic power superior to the political governments of the nation-states involved."

Further Reading: Prince, Russ Alan (July 22, 2013) Who Rules the World? <www.forbes.com>

Kurt Cobain

In the official version, 27-year-old Kurt Cobain, guitarist and frontman of the rock band Nirvana, shot himself dead on April 5, 1994. Forensics showed that he had died from a shotgun wound, which was initially reported in the press as directly to the head, but later was described as being through the mouth, after taking a large amount of drugs including heroin. However, Canadian chemist Roger Lewis makes the argument that Cobain couldn't have possibly shot himself because he had so much heroin in his system that he should have been comatose. Others suspect that his wife, Courtney Love, found out that Cobain was planning to divorce her, cut her from his will, and as a result she allegedly rendered him comatose with an injection of heroin and then shot him dead. Considering the plausible trajectory of shotgun shells, critics point out that there were no legible fingerprints recovered from the scene, and scrutinize the singer's supposed suicide note, especially the final lines which look as if they were penned by someone else.

Further Reading: Dickinson, Amy (February 20, 2013) Kurt Cobain's Final Tour. <www.esquire.com>

Big Sugar

During the 1960s and 1970s, the Sugar Research Foundation (a trade group representing the sugar industry) made an effort to refute concerns about sugar's possible ill health effects such as cancer, obesity, and heart disease. The SRF-sponsored research by Harvard scientists that downplayed the risks of sugar and highlighted the hazards of dietary fat or carbohydrates. The result was published in *The New England Journal of Medicine* in 1967, with no disclosure of sugar industry funding. As the government tried to encourage people to eat healthier, the best efforts failed for the next few decades since they were working with faulty information. The cover-up caused many Americans to suffer a variety of health problems. Sugar has been linked to higher rates of diabetes, to higher rates of depression, and is thought to be the major cause of obesity around the world. Industry advertisers find a lucrative market in Black and Hispanic communities, disproportionately targeting ads for sugary sodas and snacks.

Further Reading: Belluz, Julia (January 6, 2017) The case for eliminating sugar. All of it. <www.vox.com>

John F. Kennedy

On November 22, 1963, John F. Kennedy was assassinated, struck by two bullets, while riding in an open-topped limousine through Dealey Plaza in Dallas, Texas. Lee Harvey Oswald was charged with the crime but was himself shot dead by Dallas club owner Jack Ruby while in police custody before he could stand trial. A presidential commission headed by Chief Justice Earl Warren found that Oswald acted alone, however many believe that the federal government intentionally covered up crucial information in the aftermath of the assassination to prevent a conspiracy from being discovered. Some speculate that a second gunman —-perhaps on the grassy knoll of Dealey Plaza — participated in the shooting. Others believe in an even broader conspiracy. Countless individuals and organizations have been accused of involvement in the Kennedy assassination include the CIA, the Mafia, sitting Vice President Lyndon B. Johnson, Cuban Prime Minister Fidel Castro, the Mafia, and the KGB.

Further Reading: Bradford, Alina (March 9, 2018) Facts About the JFK Assassination. <www.livescience.com>

Global Warming

Climate change doubters believe that man-made global warming is a conspiracy designed to control the economy and impose their vision of human society through the coercive power of authoritarian government. Reduction in the use of fossil fuels, restrictions on the use of automobiles, higher taxes and forced reductions in living standards are recommended policy responses. Many believe that global warming is not about science, but about politics, expanding the power of elites using the coercive instruments of government to control the lives of people everywhere. Global warming is provided lavish support by government and taught as scientific fact in our schools, yet many believe the science has been corrupted by tens of millions of dollars provided in grants to scientists whose research supports global warming. Environmentalist groups, the UN, climate researchers and politicians have joined forces in a scam to scare people enough to make them accept more taxes on petrol and coal.

Further Reading: Kadlec, Charles (July 25, 2011) The Goal Is Power: The Global Warming Conspiracy. <www.forbes.com>

Asbestos

As far back as the late 19th century, scattered reports on the health risks of asbestos emerged in Canada, Europe and the U.S. By the 1920s, leading medical journals published articles linking asbestos to asbestosis, a new and sometimes fatal lung condition in which inhaled asbestos scars the lungs and makes breathing difficult. Yet as evidence about the harmful effects of asbestos continued to grow, the success of asbestos companies hinged on keeping its health risks a secret. Many companies took steps to ensure that miners, factory workers and the public knew nothing about the true dangers. Court evidence has revealed that multiple companies contributed to the asbestos cover-up. Some concealed medical research that may have promoted stricter asbestos regulations and safer work practices. There is still a lack of basic information about the extent to which public and private structures are contaminated by the chemical, and the government has no record of how many schools contain asbestos materials.

Further Reading: Formuzis, Alex (June 7, 2017) Asbestos Industry Covered Up Danger for Decades, and Evades Responsibility Today. <www.huffingtonpost.com>

Elvis Presley

On August 16, 1977, Elvis Presley's lifeless body was discovered on the bathroom floor of his bedroom suite at the Graceland estate in Memphis, Tennessee. An ambulance was summoned, and the paramedics, failing to resuscitate him, delivered his body to the Emergency Department at Baptist Memorial Hospital. Approximately thirty minutes later, Elvis Presley was pronounced dead, ostensibly from cardiac arrhythmia and heart disease. Yet in the days following his funeral, speculation grew among skeptics that Elvis might not have died after all. Many believe Elvis faked his own death, claiming that a black helicopter landed at Graceland hours before his body was discovered. Some claim that Elvis was the target of a criminal organization called "The Fraternity," and the FBI helped him fake his death. Among the most significant sightings, a man at the Memphis International Airport who looked a lot like Elvis gave the name "Jon Burrows," the same name he used when booking hotels.

Further Reading: McKenna, Meghan (August 16, 2017) Is Elvis Still Alive? 5 Compelling Reasons That Point to "Yes." <www.fashionmagazine.com>

PRISM

While the U.S. government is monitoring everyone's Internet usage through upstream programs, PRISM, a tool used by the National Security Agency, is more targeted. It allows NSA agents to demand data without filling out paperwork. Under the FISA act, the NSA can monitor a person's phone, email, and other communications for up to a week without going to the secret court and asking permission, and they can do it via PRISM. A lot remains unknown about how PRISM works, but the basic idea is that it allows the NSA to request data on specific people from major technology companies. Service providers who have fought these requests as unconstitutional have lost in secret courts. This surveillance program is taking place under puzzling interpretations of laws that average citizens aren't allowed to know. Data, it seems, is the modern-day Big Brother, and just about everything you do can be tracked and monitored in some form or fashion. PRISM was revealed by former CIA and NSA analyst Edward Snowden.

Further Reading: Sottek, T.C. and Kopstein, Janus ((July 17, 2013) Everything you need to know about PRISM. <www.theverge.com>

Majestic Twelve

Majestic Twelve is the code name of an alleged secret committee of scientists, military leaders, and government officials appointed by President Harry S. Truman in order to investigate the Roswell UFO incident and decide how to handle any alien incursions that might occur in the future. Members of the committee included Secretary of Defense James Forrestal, the first three Directors of Central Intelligence, an Air Force General, an Army General, the Secretary of the Army and five of America's most influential scientists — the cream of the military, scientific and intelligence communities. On May 22, 1949, when he was about to reveal his knowledge of the UFO crash, Secretary Forrestal plunged to his death from the 16th floor of the Bethesda Naval Hospital. On November 6, 1952, newly-elected Dwight Eisenhower was briefed on Operation Majestic Twelve. The briefing paper lists the 12-man committee and stresses the need to "avoid public panic at all costs," confirming that the government was covering up the truth about UFOs.

Further Reading: Dunning, Brian (July 19, 2016) The Secret History of Majestic 12. <www.skeptoid.com>

Cell Tower Radiation

The Federal Communications Commission, our government's regulating agency, does not address health concerns when cell tower applications are considered. The Wireless Association, an organization that represents wireless communications companies, states "there are no established health effects from radio frequency signals used in cellphones," despite the fact that studies have concluded exactly the opposite. Researchers have discovered a threefold increase in cancers after five years' exposure to microwave radiation from a nearby mobile phone mast transmitter compared to those patients living further away. A more recent French study found significant health effects on people living within 300 meters of mobile phone base stations, including fatigue, sleep disturbance, headaches, concentration problems, depression, memory problems, irritability, cardiovascular problems, hearing disruption, skin problems, and dizziness. More evidence is accumulating every day on the effects of electromagnetic radiation.

Further Reading: Walia, Arjun (August 17, 2018) World's Largest Study on Cell Tower Radiation Confirms Cancer Link. <www.collective-evolution.com>

DDT

Nationwide hysteria followed the publication of Rachel Carson's 1962 book, *Silent Spring*, in which she labeled DDT a dangerous chemical that might be causing cancer in humans. Experience and scientific studies have proven her wrong. On June 14, 1972 William Ruckelhaus, Administrator of the EPA, as a result of political pressure from environmental extremists, made a one-man decision to ban the use of DDT in United States, a move that was illegal. He took this action ignoring 8,000 pages of testimony and findings of most scientists and in the absence of any honest substantiating evidence. He subsequently refused to comply with requests made under the Freedom of Information Act and defied the National Environmental Policy Act by refusing to file an Environmental Impact Statement on the disastrous consequences of his decision. The pesticides that replaced DDT, such as dieldrin and aldrin, are far more toxic, and have been responsible for many deaths.

Further Reading: Waite, Donald E. Waite (November 2, 2004) Myths and Facts about DDT. <www.eco-imperialism.com>

War Against Islam

Many allege there exists a conspiracy to harm, weaken or annihilate the societal system of Islam, using military, economic, social and cultural means. The purported perpetrators are non-Muslims, particularly the Western world and "false Muslims" in collusion with political actors in the Western world. While the contemporary theory covers general issues of societal transformations in modernization and secularization as well as issues of international power politics among modern states, the Crusades are often suggested as its alleged starting point. Proponents of this view consider the "War on Terrorism," the 2001 military activity in Afghanistan and 2003 invasion of Iraq, as part of the conspiracy. Western colonialism in the Middle East throughout the 20th century is also regarded as such an attack by some. Citing attacks on minority Christians in Muslim countries, some Christian fundamentalists allege that a war against Islam is self-defense because militant Muslims "are waging war against us."

Further Reading: Journo, Elan (February 20, 2006) Exposing Anti-Muslim Conspiracies."

Barack H. Obama

The presidency of Barack Obama has spawned numerous conspiracy theories: that he was born in Kenya, that he secretly practices Islam, and/or that he is the Antichrist of Christian eschatology. A theory that came to prominence in 2009 (known as "birtherism") denies the legitimacy of Obama's presidency by claiming that he was not born in the U.S. This theory has persisted despite the evidence of his Hawaiian birth certificate and birth announcements in two Hawaiian newspapers in 1961. Other theories claim that Obama is secretly a Muslim and that he took his oath of office as a U.S. Senator in 2005 while placing his hand on a Qur'an rather than a Bible. An early version of a rumor that Obama had spent at least four years in a so-called madrassa, or Muslim seminary, in Indonesia appeared in an article published by *Insight on the News*, a magazine published by News World Communications. Although most theologians agree that Obama is not the Antichrist, they believe his policies paved the way for the Antichrist.

Further Reading: LeClaire, Jennifer (August 7, 2015) Why So Many People Think Obama Is the Antichrist.

Deepwater Horizon

There continues to be speculation about the true origin of the massive oil spill — the biggest offshore oil spill in American history — that killed 11 workers, polluted the Gulf of Mexico, and threatened marine, plant, animal, and human health in the region. Early in the investigation, *The Huffington Post* reported that oil-services provider Halliburton was a primary suspect in the accident, and drilling experts blamed flaws in the cementing process. A presidential commission later found that Halliburton officials knew weeks before the fatal explosion that the cement mixture to seal the bottom of the well was unstable but still went ahead with the job. And prior to the accident, Halliburton purchased an oil spill prevention firm that conveniently ended up working on the aftermath of the disaster. Once led by former Vice President Dick Cheney, Halliburton is often at the nexus of disaster zones. The company pleaded guilty to a criminal charge of destroying key evidence in the wake of the deadly explosion and subsequent oil spill.

Further Reading: Usborne, David (May 30, 2010) What was Halliburton's role in US oil spill?

Third Secret of Fatima

Between May and October of 1917, the Blessed Virgin Mary appeared to three shepherd children in a field in Fatima, Portugal. On July 13, 1917, Mary entrusted the children with three secrets, and two of the secrets were revealed in 1941. The first secret foretold the end of World War I and the start of World War II, and the second secret predicted the spread, then the collapse of Communism. The third secret was to be kept in the greatest confidence, and despite promises that it would be revealed to the world in 1960, the third secret was suddenly suppressed and Catholics were told it would probably remain under seal forever. Speculation of its contents ranged from worldwide nuclear annihilation to deep rifts in the Roman Catholic Church that lead to rival papacies. Under enormous pressure, the text of the third secret was officially released by Pope John Paul II in 2000, although some claim that it was not the entire secret revealed in Fatima, despite repeated assertions from the Vatican to the contrary.

Further Reading: Kosloski, Philip (May 13, 2016) 5 Surprising Revelations of the Third Secret of Fatima. <www.aleteia.org>

Big Pharma

Pharmaceutical companies do not want to find cures for diseases because they would rather make more money through chronic treatment regimens. A common claim among proponents of this theory is that big pharma suppresses negative research about their drugs by financially pressuring researchers and journals. In addition, as long as there has been research to cure serious illnesses, there have been people who believe that cures will never happen because treating diseases is simply far too profitable. They are convinced that big pharma has a vested interest in keeping herpes, arthritis, AIDS, acid reflux disease, depression, obesity, diabetes, multiple sclerosis, lupus, chronic fatigue syndrome, attention deficit disorder, and muscular dystrophy around as long as possible because peddling their treatments is far bigger business than a cure could ever be. If true, potential cures are being deliberately hidden and suppressed by the Food and Drug Administration, the Federal Trade Commission, and the major food and drug companies.

Further Reading: Haqopian, Joachim (January 18, 2015) The Evils of Big Pharma Exposed.

Tuskegee Syphilis Study

The U.S. Public Health Service conducted secret experiments, including a study on syphilis at Tuskegee University beginning in 1932. They studied 600 black men, including 399 who had syphilis and 201 who were healthy. The men with syphilis, who did not know they had the disease, were told they had "bad blood" and would be treated for it, but they did not receive treatment for syphilis. The study, conducted in partnership with Tuskegee University, lasted for 40 years. During that time, the sick subjects experienced syphilis-related health problems, but were never told they had the disease and never received penicillin, which became the recommended treatment in 1945. Researchers continued to study the natural progression of the disease until the Associated Press discovered the study in 1972 and the government shut it down. By then, 28 participants had died, and 40 wives and 19 children had contracted syphilis. The disclosure triggered belief among African-Americans that the government and medical professionals conspired against black Americans.

Further Reading: Waxman, Olivia B. (July 25, 2017) How the Public Learned About the Infamous Tuskegee Syphilis Study. <www.time.com>

GMOs

Genetically modified foods are derived from organisms which had their genomes modified using the technique of DNA recombination, and since the early 2000s, genetic modification has become a subject of intense debate. Opponents claim that production and consumption of these foods have adverse environmental and health effects, that for-profit agribusinesses like Monsanto are plotting to control the world food supply, and that they deliberately cause food shortages to promote the use of genetics, or have co-opted government agencies such as the United States Food and Drug Administration and scientific societies such as the American Association for the Advancement of Science. Resistance to specific herbicides is one of the major traits introduced into genetically modified organisms. Farmers can spray the whole field, but only the weeds will die. Yet the effects of long-term exposure to even small amounts of these pesticides have been linked to a variety of chronic health conditions such as diabetes, cancer, and neurological defects.

Further Reading: Splitter, Jenny (July 7, 2017) Why are we still debating GMOs? <www.theoutline.com>

COINTELPRO

In 1956, with the knowledge and approval of President Dwight Eisenhower, FBI Director J. Edgar Hoover authorized a covert operation that aimed to bring all the nation's counterintelligence operations together under one umbrella. The project became known as "counterintelligence program" or COINTELPRO. Over the next decade and a half, local, state, and federal agents involved in this program illegally spied on Civil Rights leaders, fabricated evidence of crimes, staged false-flag attacks, and used myriad "dirty tricks" to undermine progressive movements. Some sources claim that the FBI conducted more than 200 "black bag jobs," warrantless surreptitious entries against targeted political groups and their members. They spread misinformation about meetings and events, set up pseudo movement groups run by government agents, and manipulated or strong-armed parents, employers, landlords, school officials and others to cause trouble for activists.

Further Reading: Stockton, Richard (April 18, 2017) Domestic Spying, Blackmail, And Murder: Inside the FBI's COINTELPRO. <www.allthatsinteresting.com>

Operation Northwoods

The Cuban revolution began in July 1953, and continued sporadically until December 31, 1958, when rebels replaced the Batista government with a socialist state. Terrified by the threat of a Communist nation on America's doorstep, in the early 1960s, the Joint Chiefs of Staff reportedly drafted plans for acts of terrorism on American soil to create public support for a war against Cuba. Code named Operation Northwoods, the plans included the possible assassination of Cuban émigrés, sinking boats of Cuban refugees on the high seas, hijacking planes, blowing up a U.S. ship, and orchestrating violent terrorism in U.S. cities. The proposal was presented to Secretary of Defense McNamara on March 13, 1962, and apparently quashed by President Kennedy, leading many to speculate that it was linked to his assassination a year later. Skeptics of the official account of the September 11, 2001 attacks point to Operation Northwoods as evidence of the intent of U.S. military officials to carry out false flag operations.

Further Reading: Hunt, David (July 31, 2017) Operation Northwoods: US False Flag Attacks to Invade Cuba in 1962. <www.owlcation.com>

COPYRIGHT NOTICE

NO CRYBABIES